INTRODUCTION

In the ever-evolving landscape of financial markets, the intersection of technology and trading has given rise to a transformative force—algorithmic trading. Welcome to "Algorithm Trading: Mastering the Use of Computer Algorithms to Analyze Market Conditions, Identify Trading Opportunities, and Execute Trading Strategies in Financial Markets."

In this carefully crafted exploration, we invite you to embark on a journey that demystifies the complexities of algorithmic trading. Whether you are an aspiring trader seeking a foothold in the markets or a seasoned investor aiming to refine your strategies, this book is your gateway to understanding the inner workings of algorithmic trading and navigating the ever-shifting landscape of global finance.

Picture yourself at the intersection of innovation and opportunity. As algorithms execute trades at speeds unimaginable a decade ago and artificial intelligence unlocks unprecedented insights from vast datasets, you find yourself at the forefront of a financial revolution. The possibilities are vast, the challenges nuanced, and the potential rewards immense.

Through these pages, we will unravel the secrets behind market orders and limit orders, explore the nuances of technical and fundamental analysis, and dissect the strategies that have propelled successful traders to the pinnacle of financial success. But this journey is not only about strategies—it's a holistic exploration that delves into the critical realms of risk management, compliance, and the ethical considerations that define responsible trading in the modern era.

In the fast-paced world of finance, the ability to swiftly interpret market dynamics and execute precise trading strategies is paramount. Algorithmic trading, the marriage of sophisticated algorithms and financial expertise, has become the cornerstone of success for traders and institutions alike. This book serves as your comprehensive guide to navigating the intricacies of algorithm trading, from its fundamental principles to advanced strategies and risk management.

Embarking On A Journey Of Mastery

As you embark on this journey, we will delve into the core concepts that underpin algorithmic trading, demystifying the intricacies of market analysis, strategy development, and the intricate technology infrastructure required for seamless execution. Whether you're a seasoned professional seeking to refine your skills or a newcomer eager to grasp the fundamentals, this book offers a structured and accessible approach to mastering algorithmic trading.

Key Highlights:

• Strategies Unveiled: Explore an array of algorithmic

trading strategies, from trend-following techniques to high-frequency trading, providing you with a versatile toolkit for various market conditions.

• Risk Management Expertise: Learn the art of risk management, from position sizing to contingency planning, to ensure that your algorithmic endeavors are not only profitable but also resilient in the face of market uncertainties.

• Technology Insights: Navigate the complexities of technology infrastructure and gain insights into the programming languages and software essential for the seamless implementation of algorithmic trading systems.

• Real-world Applications: Delve into captivating case studies, unraveling the successes and pitfalls of algorithmic trading in the real world. Learn from both triumphs and challenges to refine your own trading approach.

Who Should Read This Book?

Whether you're an aspiring algorithmic trader, a financial professional looking to enhance your skill set, or an investor seeking to understand the dynamics of algorithmic trading, this book is tailored to meet your needs. The content is presented in a reader-friendly manner, combining depth of knowledge with clarity to ensure that both beginners and seasoned traders find value within its pages.

As you turn the pages, imagine the thrill of crafting algorithms that respond to market dynamics, the precision of executing trades in milliseconds, and the satisfaction of navigating the regulatory landscape with finesse. The future of algorithmic trading awaits, and with it, the potential to transform your understanding of financial markets and trading strategies.

Buckle up, for you are about to embark on a captivating odyssey through the fascinating world of algorithmic trading. Whether you're a seasoned professional or a curious newcomer, the knowledge within these pages is your compass in the ever-evolving landscape of modern finance. Let the journey begin.

CHAPTER ONE

Introduction to
Algorithmic Trading

Definition Of Algorithmic Trading

Algorithmic trading is a method of executing financial transactions using pre-programmed computer algorithms. These algorithms, often based on mathematical models and technical analysis, automatically analyze market conditions, identify trading opportunities, and execute orders with minimal human intervention. The essence of algorithmic trading lies in leveraging computational power to make swift and data-driven trading decisions.

Market Analysis: Algorithms are designed to analyze vast amounts of historical and real-time market data. They consider various factors, including price movements, technical indicators, and other relevant metrics, to form a comprehensive view of market conditions.

Decision-Making Processes: Algorithms make buy-or-sell decisions based on predefined rules and criteria. These rules can encompass a wide range of strategies, from trend-following to mean reversion and high-frequency trading.

Significance in Financial Markets

Speed and Precision: Algorithmic trading is characterized by its speed and precision. Automated systems can execute trades in fractions of a second, allowing traders to capitalize on fleeting market opportunities.

Liquidity and Market Impact: Algorithms contribute to market liquidity by facilitating efficient trading. They can also manage market impact by executing large orders in smaller, less noticeable increments.

Advantages and Challenges

Advantages of Algorithmic Trading:

Efficiency: Algorithms operate 24/7, reacting to market changes in real-time.

Reduced Human Error: Automation minimizes the impact of emotional and cognitive biases.

Data Processing: Algorithms can process and analyze vast datasets far beyond human capacity.

Challenges and Risks:

Technical Glitches: System malfunctions or connectivity issues can disrupt algorithmic trading.

Market Volatility: Rapid market fluctuations may pose challenges for algorithmic strategies.

Regulatory Considerations: Compliance with financial regulations is crucial in algorithmic trading.

Basics Of Algorithmic Trading

Algorithmic trading, also known as algo trading or automated trading, is a trading strategy that uses computer algorithms to execute pre-defined trading instructions. These algorithms are designed to analyze market data, identify trading opportunities, and automatically execute trades based on a set of predefined rules. Algorithmic trading is prevalent in various financial markets, including stocks, bonds, commodities, and currencies.

Algorithmic trading has become a significant part of financial markets, providing liquidity, improving market efficiency, and allowing for rapid execution of trades. However, it also poses challenges related to market integrity, and regulators continue to evolve their frameworks to address these concerns.

Market Analysis:

Data Collection: Algorithms rely on vast amounts of market data, including price movements, trading volumes, and other relevant information. This data is collected in real-time or near-real-time.

Technical Analysis: Algorithms often use technical indicators and chart patterns to identify potential trading opportunities. These indicators may include moving averages, the relative strength index (RSI), moving average convergence divergence (MACD), and others.

Algorithm Development:

Coding Algorithms: Traders or quantitative analysts code algorithms using programming languages such as Python, C++, or Java. These algorithms define the conditions for entering or exiting trades based on the analysis of market data.

Backtesting: Before deploying algorithms in live markets, they are often tested using historical data to evaluate their performance and effectiveness.

Execution Strategies:

Market Orders: Algorithms can execute trades at the prevailing market prices, known as market orders.

Limit Orders: Traders can use limit orders to specify the maximum or minimum price at which they are willing to buy or sell an asset.

Time-weighted Average Price (TWAP): Algorithms can be programmed to execute trades over a specified time period to achieve a specific average price.

Risk Management:

Stop-loss Orders: Algorithms often include stop-loss orders to limit potential losses by automatically selling an asset if its price falls below a certain threshold.

Position Sizing: Algorithms may dynamically adjust the size of trades based on factors such as market volatility and risk tolerance.

High-Frequency Trading (HFT):

Ultra-Fast Execution: High-frequency trading involves executing a large number of orders at extremely high speeds. HFT algorithms aim to exploit small price differentials and market inefficiencies.

Co-location: Some HFT firms physically locate their servers near exchange servers to reduce latency and gain a speed advantage.

Market Connectivity:

Direct Market Access (DMA): Algorithmic traders often use DMA to connect directly to financial markets, bypassing intermediaries and reducing order execution latency.

Machine learning and AI:

Predictive Modeling: Some algorithmic trading strategies incorporate machine learning and artificial intelligence to predict future price movements based on historical data patterns.

Adaptive Strategies: Machine learning algorithms can adapt and evolve based on changing market conditions.

Regulatory Considerations:

Compliance: Algorithmic trading is subject to regulatory oversight, and traders need to comply with relevant rules and regulations.

Market Surveillance: Regulatory bodies may monitor markets for any signs of market manipulation or abusive trading practices.

The Evolution Of Algorithmic Trading

The evolution of algorithmic trading represents a fascinating journey from manual, human-driven processes to the highly automated, technology-driven landscape we witness in modern financial markets. Technological advancements, regulatory changes, and the ongoing pursuit of efficiency and competitiveness have all shaped this evolution.

The evolution of algorithmic trading reflects the continual drive for efficiency, speed, and adaptability in financial markets. As technology continues to advance and new market opportunities arise, algorithmic trading is likely to remain at the forefront of shaping the future landscape of finance.

Let's explore the key stages in the evolution of algorithmic trading:

Manual Trading Era:

Pre-Computer Age: Before the advent of computers, trading was a manual process conducted on trading floors. Traders relied on verbal communication, paper orders, and face-to-face interactions.

Early computerized trading:

1970s–1980s: The introduction of computers marked a significant shift. Electronic trading platforms emerged, allowing traders to execute orders electronically. However, these systems were still relatively basic compared to modern algorithmic trading.

Rise of Algorithmic Trading:

Late 1980s–1990s: The emergence of sophisticated computer technology and mathematical models led to the development of early algorithmic trading strategies. Traders started using algorithms to automate certain aspects of the trading process, particularly executing large orders.

Electronic Communication Networks (ECNs):

1990s: The rise of ECNs further transformed trading. These electronic systems enabled direct interaction between buyers and sellers, reducing the need for intermediaries. Algorithmic trading began incorporating these networks for faster and more efficient order execution.

Statistical Arbitrage and Quantitative Strategies:

Late 1990s–early 2000s: Traders started using statistical arbitrage strategies, relying on quantitative models to identify pricing inefficiencies. This era saw an increasing reliance on mathematical models and statistical analysis.

High-Frequency Trading (HFT):

Mid-2000s: HFT emerged as a dominant force. Traders sought to capitalize on extremely short-term price movements, executing a large number of orders at incredibly high speeds. This phase brought a new level of sophistication to algorithmic trading, with firms investing heavily in cutting-edge technology and low-latency infrastructure.

Machine learning and artificial intelligence:

2010s–Present: The integration of machine learning (ML) and artificial intelligence (AI) into algorithmic trading became increasingly prevalent. These technologies allow algorithms to learn from data, adapt to changing market conditions, and identify patterns that may not be apparent through traditional analysis.

Regulatory Developments:

Ongoing: Regulatory bodies have adapted to the changing landscape of algorithmic trading. Various regulations aim to ensure market integrity, prevent market manipulation, and address concerns related to systemic risk associated with automated trading.

Globalization and Cryptocurrencies:

Present: Algorithmic trading has expanded globally, with firms participating in various markets simultaneously. Additionally, the rise of cryptocurrencies has introduced new opportunities and challenges, with algorithmic trading strategies extending into digital asset markets.

Significance In Modern Financial Markets

Algorithmic trading holds profound significance in modern financial markets, influencing the way securities are traded, markets are structured, and investment decisions are executed. Its importance can be understood through several key aspects:

Rapid Execution: Algorithmic trading enables the execution of trades at speeds that are impossible for human traders. This rapid execution is crucial in capturing fleeting market opportunities and responding to dynamic price changes.

Market Making: Algorithmic trading strategies, especially in the form of market-making algorithms, contribute to market liquidity. By continuously quoting bid and ask prices, these algorithms enhance the overall liquidity of financial instruments.

Smart Order Routing: Algorithms are designed to minimize the impact of large trades on market prices. Smart order routing algorithms intelligently distribute large orders across multiple venues, avoiding significant price changes caused by a single large transaction.

Elimination of Emotional Bias: Algorithms operate based on predefined rules and criteria, eliminating emotional biases inherent in human decision-making. This precision can lead to more accurate and disciplined trading strategies.

Global Trading: Algorithmic trading allows market participants to access and trade in multiple markets globally. Traders can implement strategies in diverse geographical locations without the limitations of time zones or physical presence.

Reduction in Transaction Costs: Algorithmic trading can optimize trade execution to minimize transaction costs, including bid-ask spreads and market impact. This cost efficiency is particularly important for institutional investors handling large volumes of trades.

Variety of Strategies: Algorithmic trading encompasses a wide range of strategies, from trend-following to statistical arbitrage and machine learning-based approaches. This diversity allows market participants to choose strategies that align with their risk tolerance and market outlook.

Automated Risk Controls: Algorithmic trading systems often include automated risk management mechanisms. These controls help manage risk by setting limits on trade size, monitoring for anomalies, and implementing stop-loss orders.

Algorithmic Trading Platforms: The availability of algorithmic trading platforms has made sophisticated trading strategies accessible to retail traders. This democratization of advanced trading tools empowers a broader range of market participants.

Integration of Technology: Algorithmic trading thrives on technological innovation. The continuous integration of new technologies, such as machine learning and artificial intelligence, allows algorithms to adapt to changing market conditions and discover new patterns.

Market Surveillance and Compliance: Algorithmic trading systems often come with built-in features for regulatory compliance. These features aid in market surveillance, ensuring that trade adheres to relevant regulations and preventing market manipulation.

CHAPTER TWO

*The Foundations of
Algorithmic Trading*

Understanding Market Structures

Understanding market structures is a fundamental aspect of the foundations of algorithmic trading. Market structures refer to the organization and characteristics of financial markets, and a solid grasp of these structures is crucial for traders seeking to deploy algorithmic strategies.

Types of Financial Markets:

Equities Markets

Stock Exchanges: Understanding the structure of stock exchanges where equities are traded. Different exchanges may have varying listing requirements, trading rules, and operating hours.

Fixed-Income Markets

Bond Markets: Exploring the structure of bond markets, which includes understanding various types of bonds, yield curves, and the influence of interest rates.

Derivatives Markets

Futures and Options: Grasping the intricacies of derivatives markets, including the role of futures and options in managing risk and speculation.

Foreign Exchange (Forex) Markets

Currency Markets: Understanding the decentralized nature of the forex market, currency pairs, and the impact of geopolitical events on exchange rates.

Cryptocurrency Markets

Digital Asset Markets: Recognizing the unique characteristics of cryptocurrency markets, such as decentralized exchanges and the role of blockchain technology.

Market Participants:

Institutional Investors

Hedge Funds and Mutual Funds: Understanding the Strategies Employed by Institutional Investors and Their Impact on Market Dynamics.

Retail Traders

Individual Investors: Recognizing the role of retail traders and the influence of their trading activities on market sentiment.

Market Makers

Liquidity Providers: Exploring the function of market makers in facilitating trades by providing liquidity and quoting bid and ask prices.

High-Frequency Traders (HFTs)

Algorithmic Traders: Understanding the strategies employed by high-frequency traders and their role in market liquidity and efficiency.

Market Organization:

Order Book Dynamics

Bid-Ask Spread: Understanding how bid and ask prices are displayed in the order book and their impact on trading costs.

Trading Sessions

Opening and Closing Auctions: Recognizing the structure of trading sessions, including the opening and closing auctions, and their impact on price discovery.

Clearing and Settlement

Post-Trade Processes: Understanding the clearing and settlement processes, including the role of clearinghouses in mitigating counterparty risk.

Market Regulations:

Regulatory Bodies

Securities and Exchange Commissions: Grasping the role of regulatory bodies in overseeing market activities, ensuring fair practices, and maintaining market integrity.

Compliance Requirements

Best Execution: Understanding compliance requirements related to best execution, reporting obligations, and other regulatory standards.

Market Data:

Tick Data

Price and Volume Data: Recognizing the importance of tick data in algorithmic trading for analyzing price movements and trading volumes.

Level 2 Data

Depth of Market Information: Understanding Level 2 data and its relevance for assessing market depth and liquidity.

Market Microstructure:

Price Discovery

Bid-Ask Mechanism: Understanding how prices are determined through the interplay of bid and ask orders in the market.

Market Impact

Impact of Large Trades: Recognizing how large trades can impact market prices and understanding strategies to minimize market impact.

Basics of Market Orders:Market Orders vs. Limit Orders:

Understanding market orders, limit orders, and bid-ask spreads is crucial for traders to make informed decisions and manage their trades effectively in various market conditions. Each order type serves different trading objectives and risk tolerances.

Market Orders:

Definition: A market order is an instruction to buy or sell an asset immediately at the current market price. The primary goal of a market order is to ensure that the trade is executed promptly.

Execution: Market orders are executed at the best available

price in the market. However, the actual execution price may differ slightly from the quoted price due to market fluctuations.

Advantages:

Quick execution is suitable for investors who prioritize speed.

Guarantees the execution of the order, but not the exact price.

Disadvantages:

Vulnerable to price slippage, where the executed price may differ from the expected price in volatile markets.

Lack of control over the execution price.

Limit Orders:

Definition: A limit order is an instruction to buy or sell an asset at a specific price or better. It allows traders to set a price at which they are willing to buy or sell, and the order is only executed when the market reaches the specified price.

Execution: A limit order is executed at the designated price or a better price. If the market does not reach the specified price, the order remains open until it is either canceled or the condition is met.

Advantages:

Provides control over the execution price.

It helps avoid unexpected price changes by setting predefined entry or exit points.

Disadvantages:

There is no guarantee of immediate execution, especially in

fast-moving markets.

There is a risk of the order not being filled if the market does not reach the specified price.

Bid-Ask Spread:

Definition: The bid-ask spread is the difference between the highest price a buyer is willing to pay (bid) and the lowest price a seller is willing to accept (ask) for a particular asset. It represents the cost of executing a trade and serves as an indicator of market liquidity.

Bid Price: The highest price a buyer is willing to pay for an asset.

Ask Price: The lowest price a seller is willing to accept for an asset.

Significance:

Liquidity Indicator: A narrow bid-ask spread often indicates high liquidity, meaning there is a smaller difference between buying and selling prices.

Transaction Costs: Traders aim for smaller bid-ask spreads to reduce transaction costs. Larger spreads can erode profits.

Factors Influencing the Spread:

Market Activity: Higher trading volumes generally lead to smaller spreads.

Volatility: Increased volatility tends to widen spreads.

Asset Liquidity: Less liquid assets may have wider spreads.

CHAPTER THREE

Market analysis techniques

Market analysis techniques involve the use of various methods to evaluate and interpret financial markets, assets, and securities. These techniques help traders and investors make informed decisions about buying, selling, or holding investments.

Traders and investors often use a combination of these techniques to develop a comprehensive understanding of market conditions and trends. It's essential to consider various factors and use a well-rounded approach to make informed and strategic investment decisions.

Here are some common market analysis techniques:

Fundamental Analysis:

Definition: Fundamental analysis involves evaluating a security's intrinsic value by examining relevant financial, economic, and other qualitative and quantitative factors.

Key Factors: Earnings reports, financial statements, economic indicators, company management, industry trends, and macroeconomic factors.

Purpose: To determine the underlying value of an asset and identify potential investment opportunities.

Technical Analysis:

Definition: Technical analysis involves studying historical price and volume data to identify patterns and trends that can help predict future price movements.

Key Tools: charts, technical indicators (e.g., moving averages, RSI, MACD), support and resistance levels, and trend lines.

Purpose: To analyze historical price data and make predictions about future price movements based on chart patterns and technical indicators.

Quantitative Analysis:

Definition: Quantitative analysis involves the use of mathematical models, statistical techniques, and data analysis to evaluate investment opportunities.

Key Tools: Statistical models, algorithmic trading strategies, and financial modeling.

Purpose: To analyze historical data, identify patterns, and develop quantitative models for predicting market movements.

Sentiment Analysis:

Definition: Sentiment analysis involves assessing market sentiment and investor emotions to gauge the mood of the market.

Key Indicators: news sentiment, social media sentiment, surveys, and option market sentiment.

Purpose: To understand the prevailing sentiment and anticipate potential market reactions.

Economic Indicators Analysis:

Definition: Examining economic indicators to assess the

overall health of the economy and potential impacts on financial markets.

Key Indicators: GDP growth, unemployment rates, inflation, interest rates, and consumer confidence.

Purpose: To understand the macroeconomic environment and make investment decisions based on economic trends.

Candlestick Patterns:

Definition: Candlestick patterns involve analyzing the shapes and combinations of candlesticks on price charts to identify potential trend reversals or continuations.

Key Patterns: Doji, hammer, engulfing, and harami patterns.

Purpose: To provide insights into market sentiment and potential turning points in price movements.

Cycle Analysis:

Definition: Cycle analysis involves studying recurring patterns or cycles in market movements.

Key Components: Identifying periodic highs and lows, cycle lengths, and amplitude.

Purpose: To anticipate potential turning points in the market based on historical cyclic patterns.

Intermarket Analysis:

Definition: Intermarket analysis involves examining relationships between different asset classes and markets to gain insights into potential market movements.

Key Relationships: Stock market vs. bond market; currency market vs. commodity market.

Purpose: To identify correlations and divergences that may

impact trading decisions.

Fundamental Analysis

Fundamental analysis in algorithmic trading involves evaluating the intrinsic value of a financial asset by analyzing various economic, financial, and qualitative factors. Algorithmic traders use quantitative models to process and interpret fundamental data, allowing for automated decision-making based on these analyses.

In algorithmic trading, the integration of economic indicators and financial statement analysis allows for data-driven decision-making, helping traders capitalize on market opportunities and manage risk more effectively. The ability to process vast amounts of data quickly and accurately is a key advantage of algorithmic trading in the realm of fundamental analysis.

Economic Indicators:

Definition: Economic indicators are statistical metrics used to assess the overall health and performance of an economy. Algorithmic trading systems can incorporate these indicators to gauge the economic environment and make trading decisions accordingly.

Key Economic Indicators:

Gross Domestic Product (GDP): GDP measures the total value of all goods and services produced within a country. Algorithmic models may react to changes in GDP growth rates to anticipate economic trends.

Unemployment Rates: Changes in unemployment rates

can impact consumer spending and overall economic activity. Algorithmic systems may consider employment data to assess economic conditions.

Inflation Rates: Inflation measures the rate at which the general level of prices for goods and services is rising. Algorithmic traders may adjust their strategies based on expectations of inflation or deflation.

Interest Rates: Central banks set interest rates, which influence borrowing costs and, consequently, spending and investment. Algorithmic models may incorporate interest rate data to predict market reactions.

Consumer Confidence Index: This index reflects the sentiment of consumers regarding the economic outlook. Algorithmic traders may react to changes in consumer confidence as an indicator of potential shifts in market sentiment.

Algorithmic trading implications:

Algorithms may be programmed to adjust positions or trading strategies based on changes in economic indicators.

Automated systems can quickly process and interpret economic data releases, allowing for rapid adjustments to market conditions.

Historical data related to economic indicators can be used to train machine learning models to predict market reactions to future releases.

Financial Statements and Ratios:

Definition: Financial statements provide a snapshot of a company's financial performance and position.

Algorithms in fundamental analysis analyze these statements and various financial ratios to assess a company's health and growth potential.

Key Financial Statements:

Income Statement: Details a company's revenues, expenses, and profits over a specific period.

Balance Sheet: Summarizes a company's assets, liabilities, and equity at a specific point in time.

Cash Flow Statement: Tracks the inflow and outflow of cash within a company.

Key Financial Ratios:

Price-to-Earnings (P/E) Ratio: compares a company's stock price to its earnings per share.

Debt-to-Equity Ratio: Measures a company's financial leverage by comparing its debt to equity.

Return on Equity (ROE): Indicates a company's profitability relative to shareholders' equity.

Algorithmic trading implications:

Algorithms can scan financial statements and ratios for anomalies or trends that may impact a company's value.

Quantitative models can be programmed to execute trades based on predefined thresholds for financial ratios.

Automated systems may use historical financial data to identify patterns and make predictions about future company performance.

Quantitative Analysis

Quantitative analysis in algorithmic trading involves the

use of mathematical and statistical models, as well as machine learning techniques, to analyze financial data and make trading decisions. This approach relies on quantitative methods to identify patterns, trends, and potential opportunities in the markets.

In quantitative analysis, the integration of statistical models and machine learning techniques allows for the development of sophisticated algorithms capable of handling large datasets and making nuanced predictions. These approaches contribute to the evolution of algorithmic trading strategies, enabling traders to leverage data-driven insights for more informed decision-making in financial markets.

Statistical Models:

Definition: Statistical models in quantitative analysis use mathematical and statistical techniques to analyze historical data and make predictions about future market movements. These models are based on the assumption that historical patterns and relationships can provide insights into potential future outcomes.

Key Statistical Models:

Regression analysis examines the relationship between one or more independent variables and a dependent variable. In trading, this could involve predicting an asset's price based on various factors.

Time Series Analysis: studies time-ordered data to identify patterns, trends, and seasonality. Moving averages and autoregressive integrated moving average (ARIMA) models are examples used in trading.

Volatility Models: Models like the GARCH (Generalized

Autoregressive Conditional Heteroskedasticity) model are used to predict volatility in financial markets.

Algorithmic trading implications:

Statistical models can be programmed into algorithms to make predictions about future price movements.

These models may help identify overbought or oversold conditions, potential trend reversals, or other patterns that can be exploited for trading.

Introduction to Machine Learning in Trading:

Definition: Machine learning involves the use of algorithms that allow computer systems to learn and improve from experience without being explicitly programmed. In algorithmic trading, machine learning techniques can be applied to analyze vast amounts of data and uncover complex patterns that may not be apparent through traditional statistical methods.

Key Machine Learning Techniques:

Supervised Learning: The algorithm is trained on historical data with known outcomes to make predictions on new, unseen data. Common algorithms include linear regression, support vector machines, and neural networks.

Unsupervised Learning: The algorithm explores data without predefined outcomes. Clustering and dimensionality reduction techniques, such as k-means clustering and principal component analysis (PCA), fall into this category.

Reinforcement Learning: The algorithm learns through trial and error, receiving feedback on its actions and adjusting its strategy accordingly. This approach is suitable for dynamic and changing environments.

Algorithmic trading implications:

Machine learning models can be trained to predict asset prices, identify patterns, and optimize trading strategies.

Algorithms utilizing machine learning can adapt to changing market conditions, making them more flexible in dynamic environments.

Reinforcement learning algorithms can be used to optimize trading strategies by learning from past successes and failures.

CHAPTER FOUR

Algorithmic trading strategies

Trend-Following Strategies

Trend-following strategies are a category of algorithmic trading strategies that aim to capitalize on the persistence of price trends in financial markets. These strategies are based on the idea that once a trend is established, it is more likely to continue than to reverse. Two common types of trend-following strategies are moving average strategies and breakout strategies.

1. Moving Average Strategies:

Concept: Moving averages are widely used in trend-following strategies. A moving average is a statistical calculation that smooths out price data by creating a constantly updated average price. The two most common types are the simple moving average (SMA) and the exponential moving average (EMA).

Algorithmic Implementation:

Golden Cross and Death Cross: The Golden Cross occurs when a shorter-term moving average (e.g., 50-day) crosses above a longer-term moving average (e.g., 200-day), signaling a potential bullish trend. Conversely, the death cross is when the shorter-term moving average crosses below the longer-term moving average, signaling a potential bearish trend.

Moving Average Crossovers: Traders may use crossovers between short-term and long-term moving averages to generate buy or sell signals. For example, buy when the short-term average crosses above the long-term average and sell when the opposite occurs.

Moving Average Channels: Bands around moving averages can be used to identify potential trend reversals. If prices move outside the bands, it may indicate a change in trend.

Algorithmic trading implications:

Moving average strategies are relatively simple to implement and understand.

They help smooth out short-term price fluctuations, focusing on the overall trend.

Traders may adjust the parameters (e.g., length of moving averages) to adapt to different market conditions.

2. Breakout Strategies:

Concept: Breakout strategies aim to capitalize on price movements when the market breaks through predefined support or resistance levels. The strategy assumes that once a breakout occurs, a new trend is likely to continue in the direction of the breakout.

Algorithmic Implementation:

Channel Breakouts: Identify a trading range or channel where prices have been consolidating. Buy when the price breaks above the upper boundary or sell when it breaks below the lower boundary.

Volatility Breakouts: Use measures of volatility to set dynamic thresholds. For example, buy when the price exceeds a certain percentage above its recent volatility-based average.

Price Pattern Breakouts: Identify chart patterns such as triangles or rectangles. Buy when the price breaks out above the pattern or sell when it breaks below.

Algorithmic trading implications:

Breakout strategies aim to capture strong, directional price movements.

They can be effective in trending markets but may result in false signals during periods of consolidation or low volatility.

Traders need to carefully manage risk and use additional filters to avoid false breakouts.

Both moving average and breakout strategies are popular trend-following approaches in algorithmic trading. Traders often combine these strategies with risk management techniques to enhance their effectiveness and adapt to changing market conditions. Additionally, parameter optimization and backtesting are crucial steps in developing and refining these strategies for specific financial instruments and timeframes.

Mean Reversion Strategies

Mean reversion strategies in algorithmic trading are based on the concept that asset prices tend to revert to their historical average or mean over time. Traders using mean reversion strategies anticipate that when an asset's price deviates significantly from its historical average, it is likely to move back towards that average. Two common mean reversion strategies are Bollinger bands and statistical arbitrage techniques.

Bollinger Bands and Mean Reversion:

Concept: Bollinger Bands are a technical analysis tool that consists of a middle band being an N-period simple moving average (SMA) and upper and lower bands being a specified number of standard deviations away from the SMA. The bands widen during periods of higher volatility and contract during periods of lower volatility. Mean reversion traders often use Bollinger Bands to identify overbought or oversold conditions.

Algorithmic Implementation:

Overbought/Oversold Conditions: When prices touch or move outside the upper band, it may signal that the asset is overbought. Conversely, when prices touch or move below the lower band, it may signal oversold conditions.

Mean Reversion Signals: Traders may enter short positions when prices touch the upper band and enter long positions when prices touch the lower band, anticipating a return to the mean.

Algorithmic trading implications:

Bollinger Bands provide a systematic way to identify extreme price movements.

Traders need to be cautious, as strong trends can cause prices to remain near the upper or lower bands for extended periods.

Risk management is crucial to avoid significant losses if prices continue to trend against mean reversion expectations.

Statistical arbitrage techniques:

Concept: Statistical arbitrage, also known as pairs trading or relative value trading, is a mean reversion strategy that involves exploiting short-term price divergences between related assets. The strategy assumes that the historical relationship between the assets will be reestablished over time.

Algorithmic Implementation:

Pairs Selection: Identify pairs of assets that historically have a high correlation or cointegration. This could involve stocks in the same sector, commodities, or other related financial instruments.

Signal Generation: Develop a signal to enter a trade when the prices of the paired assets deviate from their historical relationship. This could be based on statistical measures such as z-scores or cointegration tests.

Risk Management: Implement risk controls to manage exposure, such as position sizing and stop-loss orders.

Algorithmic trading implications:

Statistical arbitrage strategies aim to exploit short-term mispricing between related assets.

These strategies often involve simultaneous long and short

positions to hedge against market movements.

Careful monitoring and periodic recalibration of pairs are necessary due to changing market conditions and relationships.

Mean reversion strategies, whether using Bollinger bands or statistical arbitrage techniques, seek to profit from temporary price dislocations. Traders employing these strategies must carefully manage risk, continuously monitor market conditions, and adapt their models to evolving market dynamics. Additionally, backtesting and robust statistical analysis are crucial for developing effective mean reversion algorithms.

High-Frequency Trading (Hft) Strategies

High-frequency trading (HFT) refers to a subset of algorithmic trading that involves the execution of a large number of orders at extremely high speeds. HFT strategies aim to capitalize on small price discrepancies, market inefficiencies, and fleeting opportunities that arise within fractions of a second. Two common HFT strategies are market-making and statistical arbitrage.

Market Making:

Concept: Market making is a strategy where HFT firms continuously quote buy and sell prices for financial instruments in order to profit from the bid-ask spread. The goal is to provide liquidity to the market by facilitating trades and profiting from the spread between buying and selling prices.

Algorithmic Implementation:

Continuous Quoting: HFT algorithms dynamically adjust bid and ask prices based on market conditions, order book dynamics, and other relevant factors.

Risk Management: Sophisticated risk management algorithms monitor exposure and adjust quoting parameters to minimize the impact of adverse price movements.

Order Book Monitoring: Algorithms analyze order book data to detect changes in supply and demand, adjusting quotes accordingly.

HFT Trading Implications:

High-frequency market makers contribute to market liquidity by providing continuous buy and sell quotes.

Profits are derived from the bid-ask spread, and the strategy requires rapid order execution and low-latency infrastructure.

Market-making algorithms need to be adaptive to changing market conditions and capable of handling high order volumes.

Statistical arbitrage in HFT:

Concept: Statistical arbitrage in HFT involves exploiting short-term price divergences between related financial instruments. Unlike traditional statistical arbitrage, HFT-driven statistical arbitrage seeks to capitalize on very brief mispricing opportunities.

Algorithmic Implementation:

Pairs Selection: HFT firms identify pairs of assets with historically high correlation or cointegration.

Signal Generation: Algorithms generate signals based on

statistical measures, such as z-scores or other proprietary indicators, to identify short-term mispricing.

Ultra-Fast Execution: HFT algorithms execute trades within milliseconds or microseconds to exploit fleeting price discrepancies.

HFT Trading Implications:

HFT-driven statistical arbitrage aims to profit from rapid, short-lived pricing anomalies.

Strategies often involve complex mathematical models and advanced statistical techniques.

The success of HFT statistical arbitrage relies heavily on ultra-fast execution, low-latency infrastructure, and high-quality market data.

It's important to note that HFT strategies are subject to intense competition, and success often depends on having cutting-edge technology, co-location with exchange servers, and efficient connectivity. Due to the highly competitive nature of HFT, firms continuously invest in technology upgrades and innovations to maintain an edge in the market.

Regulatory scrutiny is another important aspect, as authorities monitor HFT activities to ensure market integrity and prevent market manipulation. HFT strategies, including market making and statistical arbitrage, have both contributed to increased market liquidity and raised concerns about potential systemic risks, requiring ongoing regulatory attention and adaptation.

CHAPTER FIVE

*Strategy Development
and Backtesting*

Identifying Trading Opportunities

The process of identifying trading opportunities is a critical step in the strategy development and backtesting process. Traders use various methods to generate signals that guide their buy or sell decisions. Two main approaches for signal generation are Technical Signal Generation and Fundamental Signal Generation.

Identifying trading opportunities through technical or fundamental analysis and subsequently developing algorithms that generate signals based on these analyses is a complex but crucial aspect of algorithmic trading. Backtesting these strategies using historical data helps evaluate their effectiveness and refine them before deployment in live markets.

Technical Signal Generation:

Concept: Technical analysis involves studying historical

price and volume data to identify patterns, trends, and indicators that can be used to predict future price movements. Technical signal generation relies on chart patterns, technical indicators, and other quantitative measures derived from historical price data.

Algorithmic Implementation:

Chart Patterns: Algorithms can be programmed to identify common chart patterns such as head and shoulders, triangles, or double tops/bottoms. These patterns may signal potential trend reversals or continuations.

Technical Indicators: Algorithms use mathematical calculations based on historical price and volume data to generate signals. Examples include moving averages, Relative Strength Index (RSI), Moving Average Convergence Divergence (MACD), and Bollinger Bands.

Trend Identification: Algorithms analyze price trends and may generate buy signals during uptrends or sell signals during downtrends. Trend-following strategies often use moving averages to identify the direction of the trend.

Algorithmic Trading Implications:

Technical signal generation is quantitative and relies on historical price data.

The choice of technical indicators and parameters can significantly impact strategy performance.

Algorithms need to be adaptive to changing market conditions and may require optimization through backtesting.

Fundamental Signal Generation:

Concept: Fundamental analysis involves evaluating the intrinsic value of an asset by examining relevant financial, economic, and qualitative factors. Fundamental signal generation relies on information such as earnings reports, financial statements, economic indicators, and company news to identify trading opportunities.

Algorithmic Implementation:

Earnings Reports: Algorithms can be programmed to react to earnings releases. For example, buying if a company beats earnings expectations and selling if it falls short.

Financial Ratios: Algorithms may generate signals based on financial ratios such as the price-to-earnings (P/E) ratio, return on equity (ROE), or debt-to-equity ratio.

Economic Indicators: Trading algorithms can react to economic indicators such as GDP growth, unemployment rates, or interest rate changes, which may impact asset prices.

Algorithmic Trading Implications:

Fundamental signal generation involves a qualitative assessment of a company or asset's intrinsic value.

Algorithms need to process and interpret a wide range of fundamental data sources.

Backtesting is essential to assess the historical effectiveness of fundamental signals.

General Considerations:

Data Quality: The quality and accuracy of historical data used in backtesting significantly impact the reliability of signals. Ensure that data sources are reputable and adjusted for splits, dividends, and other corporate actions.

Optimization: Strategies may need to be optimized for specific market conditions. Over-optimization, however, should be avoided to ensure the strategy remains robust across different scenarios.

Risk Management: Implement risk management measures to control the size of positions, set stop-loss levels, and manage overall exposure.

Market Conditions: Consider the adaptability of the strategy to different market conditions, such as trending, ranging, or volatile markets.

Transaction Costs: Factor in transaction costs, slippage, and other trading costs when assessing strategy performance.

Defining Entry And Exit Criteria

Defining entry and exit criteria is a critical aspect of strategy development and backtesting in algorithmic trading. Entry and exit criteria determine when a trading algorithm should initiate a position (entry) and when it should close that position (exit). Two important components in this process are Risk-Reward Ratios and Setting Profit Targets.

Risk-Reward Ratios:

Concept: Risk-Reward Ratio is a measure that assesses the potential return of a trade relative to its risk. It is expressed as a ratio of the expected profit (reward) to the potential loss (risk) of a trade. A common rule of thumb is to have a positive risk-reward ratio, meaning the potential reward is greater than the potential risk.

Algorithmic Implementation:

Risk Management Parameters: Algorithms set predefined levels for risk tolerance, typically as a percentage of the trading capital or as a fixed monetary amount per trade.

Profit Targets: Determine a target price at which the algorithm will take profits. This target should be set in conjunction with the risk level to ensure a positive risk-reward ratio.

Stop-Loss Levels: Set stop-loss levels to limit potential losses. The stop-loss level is triggered if the trade moves against the expected direction, helping control risk.

Algorithmic Trading Implications:

Positive risk-reward ratios are essential for long-term profitability and risk control.

Algorithms should dynamically adjust position sizes based on risk-reward ratios and market conditions.

Risk-reward ratios may vary depending on the strategy and market conditions.

Setting Profit Targets:

Concept: Setting profit targets involves establishing a specific price level at which the algorithm will automatically close a winning trade to secure profits. Profit targets are essential for locking in gains and preventing the algorithm from holding positions for an extended period, exposing them to potential reversals.

Algorithmic Implementation:

Technical Levels: Algorithms may use technical analysis to identify key support/resistance levels or chart patterns where the price is likely to reverse. Profit targets can be set at these levels.

Volatility-Based Targets: Some algorithms use measures of volatility to set dynamic profit targets. For example, a target could be a certain percentage above or below the current price, adjusting for market volatility.

Time-Based Targets: Algorithms may set profit targets based on a predefined time horizon, taking profits if the expected move does not materialize within a specified period.

Algorithmic Trading Implications:

Setting profit targets helps capture gains and prevent the algorithm from holding positions indefinitely.

Targets should be based on a combination of technical analysis, volatility considerations, and the overall strategy's objectives.

Algorithms may need to adjust profit targets based on changing market conditions and volatility.

General Considerations:

Dynamic Adjustments: Strategies should be designed to dynamically adjust entry and exit criteria based on changing market conditions, ensuring adaptability.

Backtesting: Use historical data to backtest the effectiveness of the chosen entry and exit criteria. This helps refine the strategy and identify potential pitfalls.

Consistency: Maintain consistency in applying entry and exit criteria across various market conditions to ensure the strategy's robustness.

Realistic Expectations: Set realistic profit targets and risk levels based on historical performance and market conditions. Avoid overly optimistic assumptions.

Continuous Monitoring: Regularly monitor and update entry and exit criteria based on market dynamics, news events, and other relevant factors.

By incorporating sound risk-reward ratios and setting profit targets, algorithmic trading strategies aim to manage risk and maximize returns. These considerations are integral to developing strategies that can perform effectively in various market conditions and maintain a balance between risk and reward.

The Importance And Methodology Of Backtesting

Backtesting is a crucial step in the strategy development process in algorithmic trading. It involves testing a trading strategy using historical data to assess its performance and viability before deploying it in live markets. Here's an explanation of the importance and methodology of backtesting, along with some common pitfalls and considerations:

Importance of Backtesting:

1. Performance Evaluation: Backtesting allows traders to evaluate how a strategy would have performed in the past under various market conditions. This provides insights into the strategy's potential profitability and risk.

2. Risk Management: By analyzing historical performance, traders can assess the risk-reward profile of the strategy

and identify potential weaknesses. This aids in refining risk management parameters and position sizing.

3. Strategy Refinement: Backtesting helps traders identify and rectify flaws in the strategy. It allows for adjustments to entry and exit criteria, risk parameters, and other elements based on historical data analysis.

4. Market Understanding: Analyzing historical market behavior during backtesting enhances the trader's understanding of the asset, its price dynamics, and the strategy's effectiveness in different market environments.

Methodology of Backtesting:

1. Data Selection: Choose high-quality historical data for backtesting. Ensure that the data includes accurate price information, volume, and other relevant factors. Adjust for dividends, stock splits, and other corporate actions.

2. Time Period: Select a representative time period for backtesting that includes various market conditions, such as trending, ranging, and volatile periods.

3. Modeling Transaction Costs: Incorporate transaction costs, slippage, and other trading expenses into the backtesting process to obtain a more accurate representation of real-world performance.

4. Out-of-Sample Testing: After optimizing the strategy on historical data, use a separate set of data (out-of-sample) to validate its performance. This helps assess the strategy's ability to generalize to new, unseen data.

5. Parameter Sensitivity Analysis: Conduct sensitivity analysis to assess the robustness of the strategy to changes in parameters. Avoid over-optimization by testing the strategy with different parameter sets.

Pitfalls and Considerations in Backtesting:

1. Overfitting: Overfitting occurs when a strategy is tailored too closely to historical data, capturing noise rather than genuine market patterns. It can lead to poor performance in live markets.

2. Survivorship Bias: Failing to account for delisted or bankrupted assets in historical data can result in an overly optimistic view of the strategy's performance.

3. Transaction Cost Assumptions: If transaction costs are underestimated or ignored in backtesting, the strategy's real-world performance may differ significantly.

4. Market Impact: Large trades executed by the strategy may impact market prices, especially in illiquid markets. Backtesting should account for potential market impact.

5. Changing Market Conditions: Historical data may not fully capture the impact of changing market conditions, economic events, or shifts in investor sentiment. Strategies should be adaptive to evolving market dynamics.

6. Data Snooping: Repeatedly tweaking a strategy based on historical data (data snooping) can lead to overfitting. It's essential to use out-of-sample testing and be cautious about making too many adjustments.

7. Simulation Assumptions: Backtesting relies on assumptions about order execution, fill prices, and other market factors. These assumptions should be realistic and align with live trading conditions.

8. Psychological Factors: Backtesting doesn't account for the psychological challenges of real-time decision-making. Traders should be prepared for the emotional aspects of live trading.

CHAPTER SIX

Implementation of Algorithmic Trading Systems

Technology Infrastructure

The technology infrastructure is a critical component in the implementation of algorithmic trading systems. It encompasses the hardware, software, and networking components necessary to support the rapid execution, analysis, and management of algorithmic trading strategies.

Hardware Requirements:

Low Latency Infrastructure:

High-Performance Servers: Algorithmic trading systems often require powerful servers with high processing speeds to execute trades rapidly. Low-latency servers minimize the delay between generating a trading signal and executing a trade.

Co-location Services: Traders may opt for co-location services, placing their servers in proximity to exchange servers. This reduces communication latency and ensures faster order execution.

High-Frequency Network Connections: High-frequency trading (HFT) systems require high-speed and reliable network connections to exchanges. Direct market access (DMA) and proximity hosting services help reduce network latency.

Redundancy and Reliability:

Redundant Systems: To ensure uninterrupted operation, redundant systems, including backup servers and failover mechanisms, are crucial. Redundancy helps mitigate the risk of hardware failures.

Data Backup and Recovery: Implement robust data backup and recovery procedures to safeguard critical trading data. This includes historical market data, trade logs, and strategy parameters.

Scalability:

Scalable Architecture: Design the infrastructure to be scalable, allowing for easy expansion as trading volumes increase or as new strategies are deployed. Scalability ensures that the system can handle growing computational and data storage needs.

Software and Programming Languages:

Algorithm Development and Execution:

Programming Languages: Common programming languages for algorithmic trading include Python, Java, C+

+, and R. The choice of language depends on factors such as performance requirements, ease of development, and integration capabilities.

Algorithmic Trading Platforms: Traders often use specialized algorithmic trading platforms that provide tools and libraries for developing, testing, and deploying algorithms. Popular platforms include MetaTrader, QuantConnect, and NinjaTrader.

Market Data and Execution:

Market Data Feeds: Access to real-time market data is crucial for algorithmic trading. Implement efficient mechanisms to receive, process, and store market data feeds from exchanges and other relevant sources.

Order Execution Systems: Integration with order execution systems is essential for sending orders to the market. These systems should support various order types and ensure reliable and low-latency order routing.

Risk Management and Monitoring:

Risk Management Systems: Implement robust risk management systems to monitor and control exposure. This includes setting position limits, implementing stop-loss mechanisms, and managing leverage.

Monitoring and Analytics Tools: Use monitoring tools to track system performance, detect anomalies, and analyze historical trading data. Visualization tools help traders gain insights into strategy performance and identify areas for improvement.

Compliance and Reporting:

Compliance Software: Ensure that the algorithmic trading system complies with regulatory requirements.

Implement features for monitoring and reporting trades to regulatory authorities as needed.

Audit Trails: Maintain detailed audit trails of all trading activities. This is essential for compliance, internal auditing, and resolving disputes.

Building Algorithmic Models

Building Algorithmic Models" is a crucial step in the implementation of algorithmic trading systems. This involves the development of the mathematical and computational models that define the trading strategies. Two key aspects of building algorithmic models are Coding Strategies and Connectivity with APIs (Application Programming Interfaces).

Coding Strategies:

Algorithm Development:

Programming Languages: Choose an appropriate programming language for coding the algorithmic trading strategies. Common languages include Python, Java, C++, and R. The choice may depend on factors such as ease of development, performance requirements, and the availability of libraries.

Algorithmic Logic: Code the trading logic based on the defined strategy. This involves translating the decision-making process, including entry and exit conditions, risk management rules, and other parameters, into executable code.

Backtesting: Implement backtesting functionalities to simulate the strategy's performance using historical data.

Backtesting helps assess the viability and profitability of the strategy before deploying it in live markets.

Optimization and Calibration:

Parameter Optimization: Fine-tune the strategy by optimizing parameters such as look-back periods, thresholds, and other variables. This process involves running the algorithm with different parameter sets and selecting those that result in the best performance.

Sensitivity Analysis: Assess the sensitivity of the strategy to changes in market conditions and parameters. Sensitivity analysis helps identify robust strategies that perform well across various scenarios.

Error Handling and Logging:

Error Handling: Implement robust error-handling mechanisms to detect and address issues during runtime. This includes handling connectivity issues, data anomalies, and other potential errors.

Logging: Incorporate logging functionality to record relevant information about the algorithm's activities. Logs aid in troubleshooting, performance analysis, and compliance with regulatory requirements.

Connectivity and APIs:

Market Data Connectivity:

Data Feeds: Establish connectivity with market data feeds to receive real-time price quotes, order book data, and other relevant information. Efficient data handling is critical for accurate decision-making.

Data Processing: Implement mechanisms to process and update market data in real-time. This involves parsing data, handling timestamps, and ensuring the accuracy and integrity of the information.

Order Execution Connectivity:

Order Routing: Establish connectivity with order execution systems or trading platforms to transmit buy and sell orders to the market. This requires integrating with brokers and exchanges through their trading interfaces.

Order Types: Code the algorithm to support various order types, such as market orders, limit orders, and stop orders. The choice of order type depends on the trading strategy and market conditions.

API Integration:

Broker APIs: Utilize broker APIs to facilitate the integration of the algorithmic trading system with brokerage services. API integration allows for seamless order placement, monitoring, and account management.

Exchange APIs: Integrate with exchange APIs to access trading venues and execute orders. Different exchanges may have varying APIs, and the integration process should adhere to their specifications.

Security and Authentication:

Secure Communication: Implement secure communication protocols, such as HTTPS, to protect sensitive data transmitted between the algorithmic trading system and external servers.

Authentication: Use secure authentication methods to verify the identity of the algorithmic trading system when connecting to external services. This ensures the integrity and security of transactions.

Order Execution

"Order Execution" is a critical aspect of implementing algorithmic trading systems, involving the process of converting trading decisions generated by algorithms into actual trades in the financial markets. This step aims to achieve efficient and timely order placement, taking into consideration factors such as market conditions, liquidity, and transaction costs.

An efficient order execution is crucial in algorithmic trading to translate trading strategies into actual trades with minimal market impact and optimal execution outcomes. Algorithmic execution strategies and smart order routing play key roles in achieving these objectives, leveraging automation and data analysis to enhance the effectiveness of the trading process. Continuous monitoring, optimization, and adaptation to evolving market conditions are essential for successful order execution in algorithmic trading systems. Two important components of order execution are Algorithmic Execution and Smart Order Routing. They are discussed below:

Algorithmic Execution:

Concept: Algorithmic execution refers to the automated and systematic execution of trading orders based on predefined algorithms. The goal is to optimize the execution process by breaking down large orders into smaller, manageable chunks and executing them gradually over time. This minimizes market impact, reduces transaction costs, and enhances overall trade efficiency.

Algorithmic Implementation:

Slicing Orders: Large orders are divided into smaller slices to be executed incrementally over a specified time horizon.

Participation Rates: Algorithms may dynamically adjust the participation rate to control the speed of order execution relative to market trading volumes.

Volume-Weighted Average Price (VWAP): Algorithms aim to execute trades at an average price close to the VWAP over a specified period, reducing the impact on the market.

Algorithmic Trading Implications:

Algorithmic execution strategies aim to balance the trade-off between minimizing market impact and completing the order within a reasonable timeframe.

Implementation shortfall and slippage are key metrics used to evaluate the effectiveness of algorithmic execution.

Smart Order Routing:

Concept: Smart Order Routing (SOR) is a technology that automatically determines where to route orders for execution, considering factors such as price, liquidity, and fees across multiple trading venues. The goal is to achieve the best possible execution by splitting orders across various markets and venues.

Algorithmic Implementation:

Market Data Analysis: Algorithms analyze real-time market data to identify the optimal execution venues based on factors like bid-ask spreads, order book depth, and historical liquidity.

Routing Decisions: Smart order routing algorithms dynamically route orders to different venues to achieve the best possible execution outcome. This may involve routing orders to markets with the best prices or the highest liquidity at a given time.

Fee Considerations: Algorithms may also take into account transaction fees and other costs associated with trading on different venues, optimizing the execution strategy accordingly.

Algorithmic Trading Implications:

Smart order routing helps improve the likelihood of achieving best execution by considering a range of factors across multiple trading venues.

Real-time analysis and decision-making are essential for adapting to changing market conditions and venue characteristics.

Traders need to consider regulatory requirements, exchange rules, and the overall market structure when implementing smart order routing strategies.

CHAPTER SEVEN

Position Sizing And Portfolio Diversification

"Position Sizing and Portfolio Diversification" are integral components of risk management in algorithmic trading. These concepts focus on determining the appropriate size of individual trades and spreading investments across different assets to control risk and optimize portfolio performance.

Position sizing and portfolio diversification are key components of risk management in algorithmic trading. By determining the appropriate size of individual positions and spreading investments across a diversified portfolio, traders can optimize risk-adjusted returns and enhance the overall stability of their trading strategies. The integration of these concepts is crucial for building a robust risk management framework in algorithmic trading.

Position Sizing:

Definition: Position sizing involves determining the amount of capital allocated to a specific trade or investment. It helps control the level of risk associated with each individual trade, ensuring that no single position has a disproportionate impact on the overall portfolio.

Algorithmic Implementation:

Risk per Trade: Algorithms calculate the amount of capital at risk for each trade based on a predetermined percentage of the total trading capital. This percentage is often referred to as the "risk per trade" or "risk per position."

Volatility Adjustments: Some algorithms incorporate measures of volatility to dynamically adjust position sizes. In more volatile markets, position sizes may be reduced to account for increased price fluctuations.

Optimal-F:** Optimal f is a position sizing technique that aims to maximize the growth of the trading capital by allocating a fraction of the current equity to each trade. It takes into account the historical performance and volatility of the trading strategy.

Algorithmic Trading Implications:

Effective position sizing helps manage risk by preventing the over-concentration of capital in a single trade.

Algorithms need to balance risk and reward, ensuring that position sizes align with the strategy's risk tolerance and overall portfolio objectives.

Dynamic position sizing can adapt to changing market conditions, helping control drawdowns during periods of increased volatility.

Portfolio Diversification:

Definition: Portfolio diversification involves spreading

investments across different assets or asset classes to reduce overall risk. The goal is to create a portfolio with uncorrelated or negatively correlated assets, so that the poor performance of one asset may be offset by the positive performance of others.

Algorithmic Implementation:

Asset Selection: Algorithms assess various assets and select those with low correlations to construct a diversified portfolio. This may involve incorporating assets from different sectors, industries, or geographic regions.

Risk Parity: Risk parity is a portfolio construction approach that allocates capital based on the risk contribution of each asset, rather than the traditional method of equal dollar weighting. This ensures that each asset contributes equally to the overall portfolio risk.

Correlation Analysis: Algorithms continuously analyze the correlation between different assets to identify changes in market conditions and adjust the portfolio composition accordingly.

Algorithmic Trading Implications:

Portfolio diversification helps mitigate the impact of poor performance in one asset by leveraging the positive performance of others.

Algorithms need to consider correlations between assets and ensure that diversification aligns with the overall risk management strategy.

Diversification may enhance risk-adjusted returns by spreading risk across different market opportunities.

Integration of Position Sizing and Portfolio Diversification:

Both position sizing and portfolio diversification should be integrated into the algorithmic trading strategy to create a comprehensive risk management framework.

The combined effect helps manage risk at both the individual trade level and the overall portfolio level, contributing to a more resilient and balanced trading approach.

Contingency Planning

"Contingency Planning" in the context of risk management in algorithmic trading refers to the proactive measures and strategies that traders implement to handle unexpected events, technical glitches, and extreme market conditions. It involves preparing for and mitigating potential risks to ensure the resilience and reliability of the algorithmic trading system. Contingency planning is a proactive approach to managing risks in algorithmic trading. By addressing potential technical glitches and stress testing strategies, traders and firms can enhance the resilience of their systems, minimize the impact of unexpected events, and ensure the continued effectiveness of their algorithmic trading strategies.

Two critical aspects of contingency planning are handling technical glitches and stress testing strategies.

Handling Technical Glitches:

Definition: Technical glitches can include software bugs, hardware failures, connectivity issues, or any unforeseen problems that may disrupt the normal functioning of the algorithmic trading system. Handling technical glitches involves developing protocols and procedures to quickly identify, address, and recover from such issues.

Contingency Measures:

Real-time Monitoring: Implement real-time monitoring tools to continuously track the performance of the algorithmic trading system. This includes monitoring order execution, data feeds, and system health.

Automated Alerts: Set up automated alerts and notifications that trigger when predefined thresholds or anomalies are detected. These alerts can notify system administrators or traders of potential issues promptly.

Redundancy: Introduce redundancy in critical components of the infrastructure, such as servers and data feeds. Redundancy helps ensure that if one component fails, there is a backup system ready to take over.

Failover Mechanisms: Develop failover mechanisms that automatically switch to backup servers or alternative data feeds in the event of a primary system failure. This minimizes downtime and ensures continuity.

Emergency Protocols: Establish clear protocols for emergency situations, including procedures for system restarts, data recovery, and communication with relevant stakeholders.

Stress Testing Strategies:

Definition: Stress testing involves subjecting the algorithmic trading strategies to extreme and adverse market conditions to assess their performance and robustness. This helps identify potential weaknesses, measure the strategy's resilience, and understand how it behaves in challenging scenarios.

Contingency Measures:

Market Stress Scenarios: Design stress tests that simulate extreme market conditions, such as high volatility, rapid price movements, or unexpected news events. This helps evaluate how the algorithmic trading system responds to adverse situations.

Extreme Price Movements: Stress test the strategies against scenarios with extreme price movements to assess their ability to handle rapid and unpredictable market changes.

Volume Spikes: Simulate scenarios with significant increases in trading volumes to evaluate the system's capacity to handle high transaction loads and potential liquidity issues.

Backtesting Under Stress: Perform stress testing through backtesting by applying stress scenarios to historical data. Analyze how the strategies would have performed during past stress events.

Scenario-Based Analysis: Develop a range of stress scenarios based on historical precedents and potential future risks. This helps ensure a comprehensive evaluation of the algorithmic trading strategies.

Contingency Planning Implications:

Contingency planning, including handling technical glitches and stress testing, is crucial for maintaining the integrity and reliability of algorithmic trading systems.

Regularly update and refine contingency plans based on evolving market conditions, technological advancements, and lessons learned from real-world incidents.

Document and communicate contingency measures to all relevant stakeholders, including traders, IT staff, and risk management teams.

CHAPTER EIGHT

Regulation and Compliance

Overview Of Financial Regulations

Financial Regulations in the context of algorithmic trading involves understanding the regulatory frameworks that govern financial markets and trading activities. These regulations are designed to ensure fair and transparent markets, protect investors, and maintain the integrity and stability of the financial system. The regulatory landscape varies globally, and financial institutions engaging in algorithmic trading must comply with the rules and standards set by relevant authorities. Financial regulations in algorithmic trading involves understanding the diverse global regulatory landscape and the impact of these regulations on the way algorithmic trading activities are conducted. Compliance with these regulations is essential for market participants to ensure the integrity, fairness, and stability of financial markets. Regulatory requirements evolve over time, and algorithmic trading firms must stay informed and adapt their practices to meet the changing regulatory environment.

Global Regulatory Landscape:

Major Regulatory Bodies:

Securities and Exchange Commission (SEC): In the United States, the SEC regulates securities markets, including equities and options. Rules such as Regulation NMS (National Market System) impact market structure and trading practices.

Commodity Futures Trading Commission (CFTC): The CFTC oversees commodity futures and options markets in the U.S. It plays a crucial role in regulating derivatives markets, including those related to algorithmic trading.

Financial Conduct Authority (FCA): The FCA is the regulatory body in the United Kingdom. It regulates financial markets and firms to ensure market integrity, consumer protection, and healthy competition.

European Securities and Markets Authority (ESMA): ESMA is responsible for securities regulation in the European Union. It issues directives and regulations impacting algorithmic trading practices.

Hong Kong Securities and Futures Commission (SFC): In Hong Kong, the SFC regulates securities and futures markets. It has guidelines and regulations concerning algorithmic trading activities.

Regulatory Initiatives:

MiFID II (Markets in Financial Instruments Directive II): Implemented in the European Union, MiFID II introduces regulatory measures to enhance transparency, improve investor protection, and address algorithmic and high-frequency trading practices.

Dodd-Frank Wall Street Reform and Consumer Protection Act: Enacted in the U.S., Dodd-Frank addresses various aspects of financial regulation, including derivatives trading and market integrity.

Basel III: Focused on banking regulations, Basel III aims to strengthen the stability and resilience of the global banking system. It has implications for financial institutions engaged in algorithmic trading.

Impact on Algorithmic Trading:

Compliance Requirements:

Financial regulations impose compliance requirements on algorithmic trading firms. These requirements may include pre-trade risk controls, reporting obligations, and registration or licensing mandates.

Market Surveillance:

Regulatory bodies engage in market surveillance to detect and prevent market abuse, manipulation, and other illicit activities. Algorithmic trading activities are closely monitored to ensure compliance with market integrity rules.

Risk Management Standards:

Regulations often mandate the implementation of robust risk management practices. This includes measures to address operational risk, market risk, and systemic risk associated with algorithmic trading.

Transparency and Reporting:

Financial regulations emphasize transparency in trading activities. Algorithmic trading firms may be required to disclose information about their trading strategies, order routing practices, and execution methods.

Market Access and Fairness:

Regulations aim to provide fair and equal access to market participants. Rules surrounding order types, market data dissemination, and execution practices are designed to promote a level playing field.

Impact on Innovation:

While regulations seek to address risks and protect market participants, they may also influence the development and deployment of innovative algorithmic trading strategies. Firms must navigate the regulatory landscape while staying competitive.

Cross-Border Considerations:

Algorithmic trading firms operating in multiple jurisdictions must navigate different regulatory frameworks. Harmonizing compliance efforts across borders is a challenge, and regulatory cooperation efforts are ongoing.

Compliance Practices

"Compliance Practices" in the context of regulation and compliance in algorithmic trading refer to the measures and processes that financial institutions and traders adopt to adhere to regulatory requirements. These practices are designed to ensure that algorithmic trading activities are conducted in a manner that complies with applicable laws, regulations, and industry standards. Compliance practices in algorithmic trading involve a commitment to best execution standards and meeting reporting requirements set by regulatory bodies. Financial institutions and traders must implement robust policies, procedures, and technological solutions to ensure adherence to these standards. Regular monitoring, periodic reviews, and adjustments to strategies contribute to an effective compliance framework that aligns with evolving regulatory expectations.

Best Execution Standards:

Definition: Best execution refers to the obligation of financial institutions to execute client orders in a manner that achieves the best possible outcome for the client under prevailing market conditions. For algorithmic trading, this involves optimizing the trade execution process to obtain favorable prices, minimal market impact, and timely execution.

Compliance Measures:

Order Routing Policies: Establish comprehensive order routing policies that guide the algorithmic trading system in selecting the most appropriate venues for order execution. Consider factors such as price, liquidity, and speed.

Transaction Cost Analysis (TCA): Implement TCA tools to assess the quality of trade executions. TCA helps evaluate the performance of algorithmic trading strategies, including the impact on execution costs and market impact.

Regular Monitoring and Review: Continuously monitor and review the performance of algorithms in terms of best execution. This involves assessing execution quality, slippage, and adherence to predefined benchmarks.

Documentation: Maintain detailed documentation of order routing decisions, execution policies, and procedures. Documentation is essential for demonstrating compliance and addressing any regulatory inquiries.

Review and Adjust Strategies: Periodically review and, if necessary, adjust algorithmic trading strategies to enhance best execution. This may involve optimizing parameters, adjusting risk controls, or incorporating new market data.

Reporting Requirements:

Definition: Reporting requirements in algorithmic trading involve the timely and accurate submission of relevant information to regulatory authorities. This information may include trade data, order details, risk management practices, and other disclosures mandated by regulatory bodies.

Compliance Measures:

Transaction Reporting: Comply with transaction reporting requirements by providing detailed information on executed trades. This includes data such as trade date, time, instrument, quantity, and price.

Order Book Records: Maintain records of order book activities, including the placement, modification, and cancellation of orders. These records contribute to transparency and aid in regulatory oversight.

Comprehensive Audit Trails: Implement robust audit trail mechanisms to capture a complete and accurate record of all relevant activities related to algorithmic trading. This is crucial for reconstructing events and responding to regulatory inquiries.

Regulatory Filings: Submit required filings and reports to regulatory authorities within specified timeframes. This may include periodic reports, ad-hoc disclosures, and responses to regulatory inquiries.

Compliance with Record-Keeping Rules: Adhere to record-keeping rules set by regulatory bodies. Maintain records for the required duration and ensure that they are easily accessible for regulatory inspections.

Automation of Reporting Processes:

Leverage automation tools to facilitate the efficient generation and submission of regulatory reports. Automated reporting systems can help minimize errors and ensure timely compliance.

Regulatory Relationships:

Foster positive relationships with regulatory authorities. Proactively engage with regulators, seek clarifications when needed, and stay informed about changes in reporting requirements.

CHAPTER NINE

*Future Trends in
Algorithmic Trading*

Emerging Technologies

"Emerging Technologies" in the context of future trends in algorithmic trading refer to innovative technologies that have the potential to significantly impact the landscape of financial markets and trading practices. Emerging technologies such as Blockchain and Cryptocurrencies, as well as Artificial Intelligence and Deep Learning, are shaping the future of algorithmic trading. These technologies introduce new possibilities for efficiency, transparency, and innovation in financial markets, and algorithmic traders are exploring ways to leverage their capabilities for enhanced decision-making and market participation.

Blockchain and Cryptocurrencies:

Blockchain:

Definition: Blockchain is a decentralized and distributed ledger technology that enables secure, transparent, and tamper-resistant record-keeping. It consists of a chain of blocks, where each block contains a list of transactions. Once a block is added to the chain, it is cryptographically linked to the previous blocks, creating an immutable and transparent record.

Implications for Algorithmic Trading:

Smart Contracts: Blockchain facilitates the creation and execution of smart contracts—self-executing contracts with the terms of the agreement directly written into code. Smart contracts could automate and streamline certain aspects of trading processes.

Transparency and Security: The transparency and security inherent in blockchain can enhance the auditability of trades and settlement processes, reducing the risk of fraud and errors.

Decentralized Exchanges: Blockchain technology enables the development of decentralized exchanges (DEX), where trading occurs directly between users without the need for intermediaries. This can potentially impact the structure of traditional financial markets.

Cryptocurrencies:

Definition: Cryptocurrencies are digital or virtual currencies that use cryptography for security and operate on decentralized networks, typically based on blockchain technology. Bitcoin, Ethereum, and other cryptocurrencies are examples.

Implications for Algorithmic Trading:

Increased Market Access: Cryptocurrencies provide access to decentralized markets, allowing algorithmic traders to participate in a new and evolving asset class.

High Volatility: Cryptocurrency markets are known for their high volatility. Algorithmic trading strategies that thrive in volatile conditions may find opportunities in the cryptocurrency space.

Arbitrage Opportunities: Differences in cryptocurrency prices across various exchanges may present arbitrage opportunities that algorithmic traders can exploit.

Artificial Intelligence And Deep Learning

Artificial Intelligence:

Definition: Artificial Intelligence (AI) involves the development of computer systems that can perform tasks that typically require human intelligence. In algorithmic trading, AI techniques include machine learning, natural language processing, and predictive analytics.

Implications for Algorithmic Trading:

Predictive Analytics: AI algorithms can analyze vast amounts of historical and real-time market data to identify patterns, trends, and potential trading opportunities. This can enhance predictive modeling and decision-making.

Machine Learning Models: Machine learning algorithms can adapt and improve over time by learning from data. This adaptability is beneficial for developing trading strategies that can adjust to changing market conditions.

Sentiment Analysis: Natural language processing and sentiment analysis can be used to analyze news, social media, and other textual data to gauge market sentiment. This information can influence algorithmic trading decisions.

Deep Learning:

Definition: Deep Learning is a subset of machine learning that involves neural networks with multiple layers (deep neural networks). Deep learning algorithms are particularly effective at processing and learning from complex, unstructured data.

Implications for Algorithmic Trading:

Feature Extraction: Deep learning can automatically extract relevant features from complex data, allowing algorithms to process and understand intricate patterns in financial markets.

Algorithmic Trading Strategies: Deep learning models can be applied to develop sophisticated algorithmic trading strategies, especially in scenarios where traditional models may struggle to capture nuanced relationships in data.

Risk Management: Deep learning techniques can contribute to advanced risk management by identifying potential risks and anomalies in market data.

Evolving Regulatory Landscape

"Evolving Regulatory Landscape" in the context of future trends in algorithmic trading refers to the changing and developing set of rules and regulations that govern the use of algorithms and automated trading strategies in financial markets. This landscape is influenced by global trends in financial regulation and presents both challenges and opportunities for market participants.

Furthermore, evolving regulatory landscape in algorithmic trading is characterized by global trends in financial regulation, with a focus on harmonization, market structure, technology, data privacy, and cybersecurity. While challenges such as algorithmic transparency and ethical considerations persist, there are opportunities for innovation-friendly regulations, adaptive approaches, and international collaboration to shape a regulatory environment that supports responsible algorithmic trading practices in the future.

Global Trends In Financial Regulation

Harmonization Efforts:

Global Coordination: There is an ongoing trend toward increased global coordination in financial regulation. Regulatory bodies from different jurisdictions are working to harmonize rules and standards to create a more consistent and coherent regulatory framework.

Cross-Border Oversight: Regulators are placing greater emphasis on cross-border oversight of financial activities. This includes collaboration between regulatory authorities to address challenges related to international trading activities, data sharing, and enforcement.

Market Structure and Technology:

Regulation of Market Structure: Regulatory bodies are closely monitoring and, in some cases, revising market structure regulations to adapt to technological advancements. This includes considerations for high-frequency trading, dark pools, and alternative trading systems.

RegTech and SupTech: The use of Regulatory Technology (RegTech) and Supervisory Technology (SupTech) is on the rise. Regulators are leveraging technology to enhance their monitoring, surveillance, and enforcement capabilities, and financial institutions are adopting RegTech solutions to facilitate compliance.

Data Privacy and Cybersecurity:

Focus on Data Protection: With the increasing reliance on data in algorithmic trading, there is a growing emphasis on data protection and privacy. Regulations such as the General Data Protection Regulation (GDPR) in the European Union set standards for the handling of personal data.

Cybersecurity Requirements: Regulatory bodies are imposing stricter cybersecurity requirements to address the evolving threats posed by cyberattacks. Financial institutions are expected to implement robust cybersecurity measures to protect sensitive information and maintain the integrity of their systems.

Future Challenges and Opportunities:

Challenges:

Algorithmic Transparency: Achieving transparency in algorithmic decision-making remains a challenge. Regulators are exploring ways to ensure that algorithmic processes are understandable, explainable, and not discriminatory.

Ethical Considerations: As algorithms play an increasing role in financial decision-making, there are concerns about the ethical implications of algorithmic trading. Regulators may address issues related to fairness, accountability, and the impact of algorithms on market participants.

Regulatory Arbitrage: The global nature of financial markets can lead to regulatory arbitrage, where market participants exploit regulatory differences across jurisdictions. Regulators face the challenge of coordinating efforts to minimize regulatory arbitrage and maintain market integrity.

Opportunities:

Innovation-Friendly Regulations: Regulatory bodies are recognizing the importance of fostering innovation in financial markets. Opportunities exist for regulators to create frameworks that encourage the responsible development and adoption of innovative technologies, including AI and blockchain.

Adaptive Regulation: Regulators are increasingly adopting adaptive and principles-based approaches to regulation. This allows regulations to evolve alongside technological advancements without stifling innovation, providing a more flexible regulatory environment.

International Collaboration: Collaborative efforts among international regulators can lead to the development of consistent and efficient regulatory standards. This collaboration can enhance cross-border cooperation, information sharing, and regulatory convergence.

CONCLUSION

In conclusion, our exploration of algorithmic trading has provided a comprehensive overview of the key components and dynamics that shape this rapidly evolving field. We delved into the basics of market trading, dissected various algorithmic trading strategies, and examined the critical elements of risk management and compliance. The journey took us through the foundations of technical and fundamental analysis, quantitative modeling, and the intricacies of order execution.

Looking forward, the future trends in algorithmic trading are marked by the transformative influence of emerging technologies such as blockchain, cryptocurrencies, artificial intelligence, and deep learning. These technologies present exciting possibilities for innovation, efficiency gains, and expanded market opportunities, while also introducing new challenges that demand vigilant regulatory oversight.

Speaking of regulation, our exploration of the regulatory landscape highlighted the global trends shaping the rules and standards governing algorithmic trading. The push for harmonization, increased attention to market structure, and the embrace of RegTech and SupTech underscore the industry's commitment to adapting to technological advancements while maintaining market integrity and investor protection.

As algorithmic trading continues to evolve, the ongoing collaboration between market participants, regulators, and technology innovators becomes paramount. Ethical considerations, transparency in algorithmic decision-making, and the need for adaptive regulatory frameworks are critical aspects that deserve ongoing attention.

Our journey through the intricacies of algorithmic trading has been both enlightening and forward-looking. The dynamic interplay between technology, strategy, and regulation underscores the importance of a holistic understanding for those engaged in or aspiring to enter the world of algorithmic trading. With these insights, we conclude our exploration, recognizing that the landscape will continue to shift, presenting new challenges and opportunities for those at the forefront of this dynamic and exciting domain.